A BREAK

FRANCIS DEWAR

Series Editor Jeanne Hinton

HUNT&
THORPE

Copyright © 1992 Hunt & Thorpe
Text © 1992 by Francis Dewar
Illustrations © 1992 by Len Munnik
Originally published by Hunt & Thorpe 1992

ISBN 1 85608 1110 9

In Australia this book is published by:
Hunt & Thorpe Australia Pty Ltd.
9 Euston Street, Rydalmere NSW 2116

All rights reserved. Except for brief quotations in
critical articles or reviews, no part of this book may be
reproduced in any manner without prior written permission
from the publishers. Write to: Hunt & Thorpe, Bowland House,
off West Street, Alresford, Hants SO24 9AT

A CIP catalogue record for this book is available from
the British Library

Manufactured in the United Kingdom

CONTENTS

■ INTRODUCTION

I wonder if someone has given you this book as a gentle hint? That is the spirit in which it is written, as an aside, something to reflect on now and then when you've got a moment.

It starts from the prevailing obsession with work, and achievement, and effectiveness, and speed, and efficiency. These are all good – in their place. But they can take over our whole life. Just as important are play, and being, and letting go. We need a balance –which is what this little book is all about.

Each chapter ends with a suggestion for something to do. Trying that is as much part of using this book as reading it is. May it bear much fruit for you.

Francis Dewar
Durham, October 1991

■ 1

STEP OFF YOUR TREADMILL

'WHAT ARROGANCE!' I thought to myself: 'Who does he think he is?' The intercity train had just set off when the man in the grey suit on the other side of the gangway got out his mobile 'phone and started 'phoning – loudly. In a way it didn't matter that everyone in the carriage could hear; in no way were his conversations confidential; they sounded like little more than placename dropping. Meanwhile the young couple in jeans sitting opposite him chatted quietly, a bit overawed by this important man flaunting his much travelled persona.

It felt like a parable of our life, of the exaggerated value accorded to busyness and rushing about, and of the consequent undervaluing of 'being' and relatedness. It is easy to persuade ourselves that we are not part of this, to feel superior to the man in the grey suit.

Yet he stands for a part of all of us. We are all implicated in this, because our whole society is built on the fiction that what gives us importance and value is what we do. We have lost the sense that the material world is not the whole story, that our fundamental value as persons does not stand or fall by what we achieve. We lack the sense of intrinsic personal worth that a mature religious belief provides.

■ THE NEED FOR A BALANCE

It isn't that work is unimportant or of no value. It is very necessary for the meeting of one another's needs. Any society needs the chores doing if it is to function well. And work *can* be creative and fulfilling (though in practice that is usually only for the fortunate few). But there does need to be a balance in our life both as individuals and in society between work and play, doing and being, activity and receptivity, taking responsibility and letting go. When that balance is not maintained, the importance of work gets magnified, and we are apt to load onto it all our search for ultimate significance, for personal worth, for meaning and fulfilment

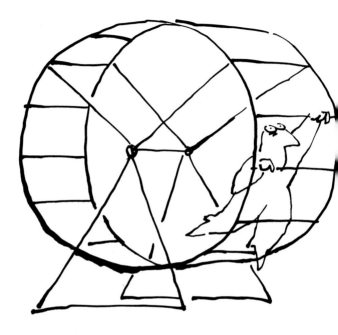

in life. This little book is about redressing this balance, and giving more importance to the neglected side of it, to playing, and being and letting go – in fact, to giving yourself a break.

I remember once seeing a demonstration of the educational methods of the Schools Without Failure Programme. Thirty or so junior school children were invited to sit on the floor and make themselves into a circle. This was done by the teacher asking *them* to see if it was a circle and to move themselves until they could see that it was. Then some discussion followed, starting from the children's feelings about school and they evolved a distinction between what they called play-work and work-work.

Many people's lives these days include no play-work at all. Life consists solely of work-work and 'recovery time' so that they can survive another large chunk of work-work. In other words, leisure has come to be thought of as mere idleness, a regrettable yet necessary need to rest and recover, for which the only justification is that it helps you to do your work-work better.

■ IT WAS NOT ALWAYS SO

What many people do not realise is that these attitudes to work and leisure are relatively recent and have only gained currency in the past four hundred years or so. For example, the peoples of ancient Greece and Rome would have taken the exactly opposite view. They would have said that you don't live to work, you work to live. Aristotle, that practical down-to-earth realist, wrote 'We are un-leisurely in order to have leisure'; and the language he spoke enshrined that attitude. In Greek, the word for work is non-leisure (*a-scholia*). It is the same in Latin (*neg-otium*). In other words, as their language reveals, they thought that leisure activities were primary, and it was work that was the regrettable necessity. The Bible takes the same view (see Genesis 3.17-19). Fortunately our present day view has not been around long enough to be incorporated into the structure of our language; though I do wonder whether our word leisure is now beginning to have overtones of idleness and time-killing rather than fulfilling and life-enhancing action and contemplation.

■ DO YOU WORK TO LIVE, OR LIVE TO WORK?

You may well disagree with me and point to the obvious fact that the majority of people do only go to work to make a living: they wouldn't go otherwise. I would not dispute that. That is certainly true of many people, perhaps the majority. But the difference in our modern attitude emerges when our income begins to increase. No matter how much it goes up we never seem to get to a point where we are content. Even if we do, our employers often drive us to put in more energy, and more hours, and more often than not we collude with that. We are all caught up in the pernicious myth that more is better, rather than being satisfied with enough.

Just to show that this is a myth and not universally true of human beings everywhere, it is interesting to see what happens when employers set up modern industrial-type organisations in overseas communities where they have not previously been known. Suppose such an employer, in order to raise productivity, introduces piece-rates, whereby workers can improve their wages, in the expectation that this will provide the labour force with an incentive to work harder. The result may be that they actually work less than before: because they are interested, not in maximising their daily wage, but only in earning enough to satisfy their

traditionally established needs (A. Giddens'
introduction to *The Protestant Ethic and the Spirit
of Capitalism* by Max Weber, London, Unwin
Hyman, 1976, p.XI). We on the other hand are
'dominated by the making of money, by
acquisition as the ultimate purpose of life.
Economic acquisition is no longer subordinated
to man as a means of the satisfaction of his
material needs' (Max Weber, same book,
page 53).

It seems that today, even if we are not all
addicted to the actual process of work itself, we
are addicted to the rewards of work, to the
status we feel it brings us; whether we regard
that as deriving from the job itself or from the
income it brings – or might bring if we worked
hard enough.

This is not the place to go into how this
change of attitude has come about. Max
Weber's fascinating book offers one view. Also
very well worth reading is *Leisure – the Basis of
Culture* by Joseph Pieper (New York, Pantheon
Books 1952). But for now I want to encourage
you to buck this trend in a practical way in your
own life. It is very easy to get sucked into the

'work for work's sake' syndrome so that you come to believe that you actually are indispensable, that unless you continuously hold up the pillars of the universe they will fall irretrievably down!

■ SOMETHING TO DO:

A workaholic friend remarked once that he was so desperately busy he was taking the evening off to go to the theatre. Take a leaf from his book. However indispensable you are, step off your treadmill for a few hours, and go and do something different. If you are always doing things for other people, or at other people's behest, do something that's for you for a change.

NOTHING DOING

A NEIGHBOUR WHO is retired says that she cannot relax without some justification. If she has not busied herself a lot during the day she feels guilty about relaxing, although she confesses that she often has to look for things to busy herself with. She is a classic illustration of what I was saying in the last chapter. Many of us function this way, and it is the very devil, a major obstacle to our relatedness, to our humanity and to our godliness. It keeps us from our families and friends, because we are too busy to have time for them: it alienates us from ourselves, because all our attention is distracted outwards: and it prevents us being open to God, because we are pulled this way and that by our over-activity.

This feature of our life today partly derives from social and economic factors, as I implied in the last chapter, and it comes out, for example, in our attitude to the unemployed. Our milkman calls once a fortnight about 4.30 p.m.

to be paid. I am the one who normally works at home and if I answer the door he always asks 'Keeping busy, then?' He never asks this when my wife answers the door! It is as though he is saying 'What right have you, a man, to be at home at this time of day? You must be skiving.' Contrary to what many seem to think, the unemployed do not need poverty to pursue them to look for work. Peer pressure and common or garden guilt about being inactive are quite enough, especially for older people. In fact this guilty fear of not pulling our weight has become so deeply and effectively embedded in our psyches that it can begin to look like a personal neurosis. 'I feel worthless unless I have work to do.' 'People will think I'm not pulling my weight unless I'm seen to be active.' 'People won't love me or respect me unless I'm always on the go.' And so on.

■ A BARRIER WHICH KEEPS GOD OUT

All this puts up an impenetrable barrier between us and God. It has turned us into people who believe we must at all times justify our existence, stand on our own feet, pull ourselves up by our boot straps. It is as though a little voice within us constantly whispers: 'You have no inalienable right to be here as part of God's creation; you have to earn your place in the scheme of things'. In fact we have ceased to believe in God for all practical purposes. We have no need of such belief. We believe in ourselves. We are the source of our salvation. We stand or fall in our own strength. No wonder we live in an age in which there is a cult of the young and the vigorous. No wonder the elderly feel unvalued. No wonder death and incurable disease are today's great unmentionables. Anything that reminds us that we are mortal, that we are vulnerable, weak, helpless and dependent is anathema and must be brushed briskly under the carpet. If I trust in my own strength in everything, I leave no room for God: I play at being God myself. I walk tall in my own self-importance, armoured against the slings and arrows of outrageous fortune by my six figure income and my private health insurance.

But consider for a moment. When you see the important business executive hurtling down

the motorway in his big Mercedes to get to the meeting in Leeds on time, reflect that what they will be discussing is the vital question of how to alter the recipe of the batter on the frozen fish because it is not selling well, or how to modify the cut of next year's suits in order to persuade us to replace the perfectly good ones we already have.

■ THE LONGING FOR TIME TO LIVE

Thomas Merton writes:

A great deal of virtue and piety is simply the easy
price we pay in order to justify a life that is
essentially trifling ... In our society, a society of
business rooted in puritanism, based on a pseudo-
ethic of industriousness and thrift, to be rewarded
by comfort, pleasure, and a good bank account, the
myth of work is thought to justify an existence that
is essentially meaningless and futile. There is, then,
a great deal of busy-ness as people invent things to
do when in fact there is very little to be done. Yet
we are overwhelmed with jobs, duties, tasks,
assignments, 'missions' of every kind. At every
moment we are sent north, south, east, and west by
the angels of business and art, poetry and politics,
science and war, to the four corners of the universe
to decide something, to sign something, to buy and
sell. We fly in all directions to sell ourselves, thus
justifying the absolute nothingness of our lives. The
more we seem to accomplish, the harder it
becomes to really dissimulate our trifling, and the
only thing that saves us is the common conspiracy
not to advert to what is really going on.

No matter how empty our lives become, we are
always at least convinced that something is
happening because, indeed, as we so often
complain, too much is happening. There is so
much to be done that we do not have time to live
... Such is the cliché.

But it is precisely this idea that a serious life

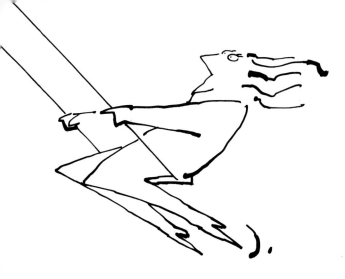

universally-shared sense of the rhythm of ordinary days and festival days, of working days and days to celebrate the gift of life; no communal or public sense of the need to worship God and to acknowledge that he, and not we ourselves, is the source and the goal of all our hopes and longings, that the gift of life is in his hands, not ours.

■ MAKING A STAND

In the face of this, perhaps all most of us can do is to make some small stand against it in the ordering of our own life. But it is difficult to swim against the current, as I have found myself. In 1988 I wrote:

It is now six and a half years since I started out on the Journey Inward, Journey Outward Project (on vocation and spiritual direction, helping people to link prayer and action in their lives). For some time I have had the feeling of repeating myself in the courses and things that I run. I badly need to stand back and have a time of being, of mulling, of reading, of sabbatical or semi-retreat. I like the story told by Frances Wickes (*The Inner World of Choice*, Boston, Sigo Press, 1988, p.64) of the woman travelling in India who chanced on a maker of brass bowls. She picked up one of intricate design and asked its price. "Two annas". She thought of a friend who ran a 'gifte shoppe' in America and of the profit she could make. "Ask him", she said to the interpreter, "how much will they be if I take fifty like this?" The maker pondered. "Four annas". "But", said the bewildered woman, "tell him if I take so many they must be less, not more". The craftsman answered, "tell the lady that if I repeat myself so many times, I must have much money, for I shall need to go away in solitude so that my spirit can recreate itself". Some time ago, it got to that point with me. I know in my heart that I need this time, and I have taken steps to arrange it: yet how difficult it is to live it. The pull of society's attitudes is so strong upon me, both within as well as without.

For me there is also a practical matter that lends its strength to that pull: the fact that if I do less, I bring less income in. There is also the fear that if I do less, the Project will somehow wither. People sometimes ask, "Are you keeping busy?" That raises my demons all right! I want people to think that I am, or they might think that the Project is not 'succeeding'. But in my heart I know that being busy, and especially giving the impression of being busy, is a kind of betrayal of what I am about. But how hard it is not to fall into this way of thinking! It was easier in the first few months after resigning my parish (I was an Anglican parish priest for twenty-one years, until the end of 1981). But now, after six and a half years, when it might be expected that I've 'got somewhere', it's much more difficult.

That was a stage in my own life when I needed a more extended period of sabbatical time. We'll come to that possibility later. For now, let me suggest a more modest aim.

■ SOMETHING TO DO

Arrange to have a day of sabbath time. On this day do everything slowly and deliberately and with mindfulness. Only do chores that are really necessary, and do them slowly, being present to what you are doing.

At some stage have a leisurely bath, conscious at every moment of what you are doing, and of what your five senses communicate to you, the smell of the soap, the feel of the water lapping your body, the sounds of rippling and splashing; and so on.

At some point go for a walk, but not a strenuous one. Let it be a stroll, such as I outlined in chapter 3, with as much awareness as you can of your surroundings and of your own physical sensations as you move your limbs.

Have a time of stillness sometime in the day, when you sit yourself down to be attentive and silently present to your surroundings, and allow the contentment and gratitude in your innermost being to rise towards God. (This might happen also at other times during the day.)

It may be that slowing your pace in this kind of way makes you aware of how tired you are. Lie down and rest, if you need to.

If you have the opportunity to attend a church service, do so with simple awareness of all that is happening. If you find yourself feeling critical of anything, set aside any critical thoughts. Simply allow to be what is. Do not on any account undertake any duties in connection with the conduct of the service. Just be there quietly without responsibility.

It may be that it is simply impossible for you to have a day like that at home. You may need to go away for twenty-four hours to make it possible. If so, go somewhere where you can be quiet, and where demands will not be made on you. A retreat house is a possibility for this (see page 48).

6

THE SEARCH FOR SILENCE

Thomas Merton writes:

EVERYONE NEEDS ENOUGH silence and solitude in their lives to enable the deep inner voice of their own true self to be heard at least occasionally. When that inner voice is not heard, when man cannot attain to the spiritual peace that comes from being perfectly at one with his own true self, his life is always miserable and exhausting. For he cannot go on happily for long unless he is in contact with the springs of spiritual life which are hidden in the depths of his own soul. If man is constantly exiled from his own home, locked out of his own spiritual solitude, he ceases to be a true person. He no longer lives as a man. He is not even a healthy animal. He becomes a kind of automaton, living without joy because he has lost all spontaneity. He is no longer moved from within, but only from outside himself, he no longer makes decisions for himself, he lets them be made for him. He no longer acts upon the outside world, but lets it act upon him. He is propelled through life by a series of collisions with outside forces. His is no longer the life of a human being, but the existence of a sentient billiard ball, a being without purpose and without any deeply valid response to reality.

(*The Silent Life*, London, Sheldon Press, 1975, p.167)

That was written in the days before inclusive language became an issue. I hope that you will be able to see past Merton's use of 'he 'and 'him', that he is speaking for women just as much as men.

In this chapter I want to commend to you the possibility of going on a retreat. By this I mean a few days away to be with God, with others and with yourself in silence. If you have never tried it, this may sound a bit daunting.

'How on earth will I survive without talking for two or three days? Won't it feel very odd being with other people and eating meals together without saying anything? And what on earth will I do all day? These are natural fears and hesitations. All I can say is that for most people they are soon allayed, and they find the experience very beneficial.

■ WHAT A RETREAT IS FOR

In general the aim of a retreat is to stand back from your normal active life of work and relationships and give yourself some more extended sabbath time, a time to be present and open to God in an unhurried way in pleasant and restful surroundings. The outer silence of the lips is intended as an aid to make more possible the much more difficult inner silence. Do not be discouraged if in the first hours, or even days, of a retreat you find that refraining from talking makes you aware of incessant chatter and activity in your mind. That is what most people find. The discipline of being present, of being aware of your surroundings and your sensations in the kind of way that I have already described, is a good antidote to this. But do not worry if you find you are only able to maintain this awareness for a few minutes at a time, before the inner chat show starts up again. Be very patient with yourself. But if you persevere gently, you may perhaps begin to be aware of a deep silence, both within you and in the world around you, as it were beneath and beyond the surface of things, the eternal pregnant stillness that is the creative and loving presence of God.

■ DIFFERENT KINDS OF RETREAT

What do you do all day on a retreat? When I
first started going on retreats in the 50s they
took the form of what are now called preached
retreats. They were usually held in country
houses which had been bequeathed to the
Church and adapted for this purpose and would
accommodate about thirty people. Each day
there would be a programme of four or five
services in the chapel, plus a couple of addresses
by the conductor, a clergyman specially invited
to lead the retreat. In between the fixed points
you were left very much to your own devices.
People would read, or pray, or snooze, or go for
a walk. The conductor would be available to
individuals for private consultation if you
wished.

This kind of retreat is still widely available. It
is very helpful for people who like a ready-made
structure to their day, and as long as you can
cope with being in silence for two or three days
on end without much guidance as to how to use
it, it's fine. A critic might say it suits the sort of
people who like to hide behind the paper at
breakfast: it gives you permission to be like that

all day! Looked at positively, it can be very therapeutic for people whose lives are over busy and full of hassle and responsibility. It provides an outline structure, with spaces between, and makes the minimum of demands on the retreatants.

At the opposite end of the scale is what has come to be known as the individually guided retreat, or IGR for short. These originated with the Jesuits, and the approach is usually (though not always) based on the exercises of St. Ignatius Loyola. They usually last for eight days, unless you decide to do the full exercises which take thirty days. There is a minimum of set structure on this kind of retreat. In fact often the only structure is the mealtimes and the eucharist at mid-day each day, and a half hour daily meeting with a personal guide who will encourage you to set your own programme of prayer times and will offer you passages from the Bible to use as the basis for your praying. This sort of retreat can be quite hard work, emotionally if not in other ways, and will involve you in several hours of praying on your own each day.

In between these extremes there have grown

up more recently all kinds of different sorts of retreats, some in total silence, others with varying amounts of quiet, some very activist, some with very little set structure, some with individual guidance, some without. Some are built round activities, like painting, or music-making, or modelling clay, or calligraphy, or story-telling: these are suitable for people who like to have something to do as a way into

prayer and self-awareness before God.

It is also possible to make what is called a private retreat, which you arrange yourself, and not as a member of a conducted group. You can do this at most retreat houses, and also at some convents and monasteries. The advantage of the latter is that there is a ready-made structure of corporate worship that you can join in as much or as little as you need to. If you do make a private retreat, however, it is as well to arrange to have someone you can consult with when you need to. The journey into God in silence is not always plain sailing, and most of us need wise guides.

■ SOMETHING TO DO

Go on a retreat. *The Vision*, the journal of the ecumenical National Retreat Association, lists all kinds of retreats and retreat houses all over Britain. It is obtainable from The National Retreat Centre, 24 South Audley Street, London W1Y 5DL. As I have already explained, retreats vary a great deal these days. Before finally deciding on one, it is a good idea to ring up and find out more specifically what form it will take. Will it be in silence (some so-called retreats nowadays are full of activity, and some may have very little time in silence)? How much will it be geared to the needs of each individual? Will there be adequate guidance for first-time retreatants? Or any other queries you may have.

7

THE STUFF OF DREAMS

IMAGINE THAT AN unknown benefactor has made a bequest to you of a large sum of money. There is a condition attached: you must take twelve months' leave of absence from your work, and be free of all obligations which you feel might tie you. But there are no preconditions whatsoever about how you spend the time. If you decide to spend six months of it lying on a beach in the Bahamas, there is no reason why you shouldn't. And it will be possible for rules which might stand in the way of your plans to be temporarily suspended. How will you spend your twelve months?

If you ask people this sort of question, answers seem to fall into roughly three categories: doing things they've dreamed of doing; putting their feet up or being cared for; and travelling. Some people have dreams of things they would love to do if only they had the time or the money. One would run fun-days for adults and children in order to help adults to learn to play. Another would take singing lessons. Another would write a book. Another would start a gardening co-operative. And so on.

A second group of people will say things like 'be looked after in a hotel', or 'spend two months in a croft on the Hebrides in Scotland', or 'get myself some counselling or help with personal growth'. These people don't know what they want to do until they've had a chance to rest and to reflect. They are so pulled this way and that by the demands of their families or their work that they've lost touch with their inner selves.

A third group want to travel, round the world, or to China, or to visit base communities in South America, or to walk the journeys of St. John of the Cross in Spain. Often this kind of travelling is a prelude to, or a substitute for, another kind of travelling, the personal journey of faith, or of a change of direction of some sort. For example, in 1977 I found myself thinking that seventeen years after my ordination it would be interesting to visit some of the people

I had been at college with to see how their views about ministry had changed. As the idea developed, it eventually took the form of a week away talking to all sorts of people, not just clergy; and I began to realise on my return that my little expedition had been an exploration of how *my* views were changing. Some years later it became apparent that it had been one step along the road to resigning from parish work and starting out on a project of my own.

■ A MORE ACTIVE SABBATH TIME

In a previous section we thought about sabbath in its primary sense of desisting from work. Now I want to turn your thoughts to a more active kind of sabbath time, what has come to be called the sabbatical. I believe this originated in the modern era in the 1890s in American universities with the custom of teachers taking time off for study or travel for one year in every seven. The notion of one year in seven for the sabbatical comes from Leviticus:

> When you enter the land which I am giving you, the land must keep sabbaths to the Lord. For six years you may sow your fields and prune your

vineyards and gather the harvest, but in the seventh year the land is to have a sabbatical rest, a sabbath to the Lord. You are not to sow your field or prune your vineyard; you are not to harvest the crop that grows from fallen grain, or gather in the grapes from the unpruned vines. It is to be a year of rest for the land.

(Leviticus 25.2-5).

Just as the fruitfulness of the land requires fallow time, so does the creativity of the mind and heart.

Since 1900 the practice has spread, though it is still mostly confined to academic jobs, and often for a shorter period than a year. But the notion of sabbatical time for study or research or further training has begun to spread beyond the groves of academe. I would like to widen the notion still further and recommend it to everyone as a time for doing what you long to do but feel you don't have the time for in the ordinary whirl of weeks and years. For the purpose of this little book, let 'sabbatical' mean a time for doing what you would love to do rather than merely desisting from what you dislike doing, a time for fulfilling activity and not just recovery from the treadmill.

■ LIVING YOUR GIFT

For their soul's health, everyone needs an opportunity now and then to take wings and fly, to do something that gives expression to the gift that is in them which is not called forth in their ordinary life and work. For the world's health, too, we need that. How much richer would all our lives be if people around us at home and at work were doing things they love to do.

There's nothing like that for spreading good humour and creativity and love. Other people's flourishing affects all of us, just as other people's misery and soulless soldiering does, to say nothing of the practical contribution to the life of the world when people's giftedness is given expression. In saying that I don't mean Giftedness with a capital G. I believe that every human being has the potential to be a gift in enacting their unique aptitudes. I would go further and say that at each stage of life God calls everyone to some task which not only gives expression to their uniqueness, but which furthers his continuing creative work.

Gerard Manley Hopkins put it well in his sonnet *As Kingfishers Catch Fire* …

> Each mortal thing…
> Deals out that being indoors each one
>   dwells …
> Crying *what I do is me: for that I came.*
> I say more: the just man justices; …
> Acts in God's eye what in God's eye he is –

Christ - for Christ plays in ten thousand
  places,
Lovely in limbs and lovely in eyes not his
To the Father ...

He expresses so well how each earthly object
and creature needs to enact its uniqueness, to
give expression to what he calls its inscape, its
inmost being. In Hopkins' view that is also to
express its Christness, its God-nature.

■ ACTING CONTRARY TO THE TRUTH OF YOUR CONDITION

In reality Hopkins' unique vocation was as a
poet. But, sadly, like many Christians, he did
not see that as a calling from God. He was
imprisoned, like so many even today, by the
disabling notion that God's calling is confined to
priests and monks. He was both, and there were
times in his life when he gave up writing poetry
because he felt it pulled him away from his
'vocation'. What soul-murdering damage can be
done sometimes in the name of religion! And
how important it is to look beyond religion to
the living, loving and lifegiving God!

  Hopkins' biographer Robert Bernard Martin
chronicles the depressive moods to which his

subject was prone for much of his life and which in the end literally crushed the life out of him. Martin does not say so, but it sounds as if there was a strong element of what the ancients called accidie in Hopkins' life. Thomas Merton writes:

'The sense of loss, forsakenness and abandonment by God comes particularly to the man who is acting contrary to the truth of his condition';

in Hopkins' terms, to the just man who does not justice or to the poet who tries to ignore or suppress his muse. Merton points to the

… infidelity to a personal demand of which one is at least dimly aware: the failure to meet a challenge, to fulfil a certain possibility which demands to be met and fulfilled. The price of this failure to measure up to an existential demand of one's own life is a general sense of failure, of guilt. And it is important to remark that this guilt is real, it is not necessarily a mere neurotic anxiety. It is the sense of defection and defeat that afflicts a man who is not facing his own inner truth and is not giving back to life, to God and to his fellow man, a fair return for all that has been given him.

(*Contemplative Prayer*, London, DLT, 1973, p.121)

It was this that afflicted Hopkins, and it lurks in the recesses of many hearts today. It is to escape this that many people today take flight into hard work. Writing of this same accidie, known to the ancients as one of the seven cardinal or root sins, Josef Pieper notes that

> it is the source of many faults and among others of that deep-seated lack of calm which makes leisure impossible ... Leisure is only possible when a man is at one with himself, when he acquiesces in his own being, whereas the essence of accidie is the refusal to acquiesce in one's own being.
> (*Leisure, the Basis of Culture*, New York, Pantheon Books, 1952, p.40)

■ A PERSONAL CALLING

All of this is to begin to speak of the importance of responding to God's personal calling to you, of how vital it is that you live out your inmost truth and in doing so allow yourself to be fashioned into one of God's gifts to the world (See my *Called or Collared? an alternative approach to vocation*, London, SPCK, 1991 and *Live for a Change, discovering and using your gifts*, London, DLT, 1988). I love that saying of St. Irenaeus: 'offer your heart to God in a soft and tractable state, that you may receive the impress of his fingers, lest being hardened you should escape his workmanship and your life'. The metaphor is of the potter (cf. Jeremiah 18 and Isaiah 45.9 and 64.8). He fashions us, not out of nothing, but from the clay and the mud of our own personal history, that unique bundle of wounds and possibilities that each one of us is. And, if we will let him, he creates a vessel that has a beauty all its own, to be a gift to others, and a utensil in God's kingdom work.

So a sabbatical time could be a time to listen more carefully to your inner truth, to allow the gentle and deft hands of the potter to do a little more work on his precious vase, to allow yourself to enact a little more of your hidden possibilities.

■ SOMETHING TO DO

If you have read this far, you may be thinking 'no way have I time or resources to take a sabbatical'. I am not suggesting at this point that you should: but I am going to suggest that you plan one. Give some time to daydreaming what you'd love to do if you had the opportunity. Don't worry about it having to be a self-improving or world-improving activity. The chief criterion is that it is something you would love to do.

8

TAKE WINGS

AS YOU READ the previous chapter you may now and then have felt, 'What's the use of all this daydreaming? I don't have the remotest chance of doing anything about it'. The use of it is that it begins to put you in touch with the inner sources of your God-given energy. The secret of getting anything done that is remotely innovative, life-changing or creative is to be in touch with God in your deepest self. Insofar as what you do flows from what you deeply are it is always fruitful. God invites you to that in some respect at each stage in your life. And whatever the difflculties, you will find that they will not grind you down. As Isaiah says:

> He gives vigour to the weary, new strength to the exhausted. Young men may grow weary and faint, even the fittest may stumble and fall; but those who look to the Lord will win new strength, they will soar as on eagles' wings; they will run and not feel faint, march on and not grow weary.
> (40:29–31)

But in order to give yourself a chance to be in touch with that inner spring you need to give yourself permission to dream, without trammelling the process by requiring every idea to be practical or possible. If you hedge your imagination about with 'buts' – 'that's an interesting possibility, but …' – it will never take wings. God cannot show you even a glimpse of the promised new land if you insist on keeping the eyes of your heart tight shut.

However, let's assume that you have been able to do a little dreaming of dreams, that you have been able to plan some sabbatical time, at least in imagination. The next step is to think about ways of making it possible. This may well raise a crescendo of 'buts' in your mind.

1. 'They can't possibly manage without me.'
2. 'I can't afford it'.
3. 'I couldn't square it with my conscience'.
4. 'I'll lose out on the ladder of promotion'.
5. 'I daren't'.
6. 'How will I explain it to my boss / spouse / dog / neighbours', etc.?

■ POSSIBLE APPROACHES

Let me offer some possible approaches to each of these obstacles,

1. Give a bit of thought to how it might be possible to get your duties covered. Or is it time for a change of job anyway? If it is really impossible, consider a shorter period for your sabbatical; say, six months, or even two months.

2. Try changing that to 'I choose not to afford it'. To what extent are your spending patterns

or life-style really unalterable? Or would it be truer to say that they are the results of choices you have made which you are unwilling to regard as negotiable?

3. Is it your conscience? Or just the condemning little imp inside you who whispers that it's sinful to do what *you* want?

4. If the ladder of promotion is of overriding importance to you, this book is not for you and should be consigned to the bin forthwith.

5. Welcome to the company of the fearful! For if we face our fear, the Kingdom of Heaven is ours.

6. You may have a job doing so. And in the end if they don't understand, perhaps it's their problem more than yours?

■ SOMETHING TO DO

Start making preliminary arrangements to take your sabbatical.

And when you finally take your sabbatical, have the time of your life!